"There was a feeling of 'yes-I-want-to-change-the-world' in the air and it's hard to imagine anyone left feeling angry or depressed about social injustice, since the performers conveyed their social agenda with just the right amount of optimism and hopefulness."

Irina Jauhianinen, Sabotage Reviews

"She Grrrowls is a ravishing, fierce and funny showcase of the some of the best mouths in town."

Amber Tamblyn

ANTHOLOGY

Edited by
Carmina Masoliver

Burning Eye

BurningEyeBooks
Never Knowingly
Mainstream

This edition published by Burning Eye Books 2017

www.burningeye.co.uk
@burningeyebooks

Burning Eye Books
15 West Hill, Portishead, BS20 6LG

ISBN 978-1-911570-14-1

For Girls with Grrrowl

CONTENTS

INTRODUCTION

Boys and girls

She had a beautiful ~~mind~~ smile. ~~His~~er ~~grades~~ teeth
were straight ~~As~~ and she was destined for bright
things. She played ~~football~~ the piano and you
could hear the sweet sound of ~~victory~~ her voice
for miles when she ~~scored a goal~~ sang. When she
was older she wanted to be a lawyer's housewife.
She had traditional values. She believed it was
more important for ther ~~mother~~ to be there for the
children than have a career. The people on TV and the
magazines say it like it is: you can't have it all
if you're a woman. It was ~~his~~er goal to find a good
~~university~~ man to ~~study law~~ start a family with.
~~When~~ she ~~was~~ould probably go for an older man ~~he'd~~
~~think about relationships~~ who was ready to settle
down; there was no time ~~for that later~~ to waste.

She Grrrowls started out as a Feminist discussion and zine-making group that never really took off. Thankfully, it has seen more success as a live literature event, which features women in poetry, comedy, music and anything in-between. It can be a struggle for anyone running an independent arts night, yet due to this remit, it is mostly women who attend the event, it has been in three different venues in under two years, and there has been some "what about the menz?" backlash. Although this latter point has been minimal, I still worry – anxious, shy-girl that I am – that others harbour unexpressed negative thoughts for my desire to create a platform that focuses on women.

One of the points that has been raised by critics is that it is well-known that music and comedy can be a battle against sexism and misogyny. But surely not poetry? There are facts and statistics within poetry publishing that prove otherwise, and on the Burning Eye Books website last year it was acknowledged: "Today we have seen a poetry event for International Women's Day where two of the three headliners are male and the line up for the poetry stage at a major UK festival has a disappointing 19 male to 5 female performer ratio."

More than that, the poetry scene is a microcosm of the world, and it has its fair share of sexist and misogynist content. It is difficult, and not always presumably safe, to speak out at events when this happens. I admit, at times I even worry about speaking out for fear of patriarchy putting me into a box that labels me as something one-dimensional before calling me a human.

She Grrrowls is not perfect, but it strives simply to showcase women and carve out a safe space with clear values set out in its manifesto, where trans-inclusion, and intersectionality as a whole, is held to high regard. Dedicated to 'Girls with Grrrowl', this is meant as a message of empowerment for young women who maybe, like me, have been told they will never be the life and soul of the party. For those who have some 'grrrowl' in them, even when those around them can't see it.

Throughout its time I have tried to gain as much feedback from audience members as possible, and with a planned run at Edinburgh Fringe Festival 2017, I hope to make She Grrrowls even bigger and better. Yet, I wouldn't be writing this if it wasn't for the rest of the team: Rowena Knight, whose poem follows this introduction; Julia Watson; comedian and zine-editor; and Christina Lappia, who I met at a festival and has been a dedicated team member since the start.

In this collection, I have selected ten poets who have featured at She Grrrowls in the past between September 2013 and November 2014 since gaining funding from Ideas Tap in 2015. Each writer was commissioned to write one poem, which sits within each individual chapter, alongside beautiful illustrations by Natalie Cooper.

It has been so exciting to see the work that has been produced and I'm so proud of each and every person that makes up this collection – full of power, passion and panache!

Carmina Masoliver
Founder of She Grrrrowls

Please note some content includes references to sexual violence, abuse and mental health issues. Some readers may find certain poems triggering.

Made.com

I ordered a couch with slender legs, soft
as a girl, with the feel of an earlobe
or peach. The colour of naked, of cream
left out, a cat's tongue lapping the light.

A couch for buttered Sundays, smooth white wine,
for leaving bills to crinkle and yellow.
A couch for entertaining Marcia,
for her gold legs to unfold and open.

Imagine my horror when I tugged free
the last piece to find a woman, flat-packed
at the back. Polished and white as a sink,
she's hat-stand tall, and doesn't say a word.

She's quite the thing next to the piano,
one arm half-raised, as if about to speak.

Rowena Knight

AISLING FAHEY

Aisling was Young Poet Laureate for London 2014/15, completing residencies at the Free Word Centre, the London Irish Centre and the Olympic Park, amongst others. She has performed across the UK and internationally, including Ireland, America and India. She has appeared on Front Row, BBC Radio 4, BBC London and ITV London Tonight.

Applying Mascara at Euston

I am sat between two women
doing their make-up on the tube.
I never thought I'd be the kind of woman
to do my make-up on the tube,
maybe I never will, but right now
I am between them both.

I imagine a life in which I am so well put together
I see the benefits of applying make-up on the move.
Blush swept across cheeks as train jerks,
eye liner drawn whilst train stands still at Kings Cross,
all for an extra five minutes in bed.

Alas, I have the extra five minutes anyway,
apply my make-up in the mirror, stood still,
arrive at my destination, only minutes
after I'm supposed to.

Interview, February, 11.30 - West Ken.

I am the kind of girl
who goes to interviews in West Kensington,
who wears a coat too light for this weather
this one time
to impress
even though I'd much rather them like me
having seen my shabby,
oversized coat
that keeps me warm.

Eyebrow Bar, Selborne Walk

You too can be the girl who gets your eyebrows done on
    Saturdays.

I like to make sure my conversations pass the Bechdel
    Test,
but on Tuesdays we talk about boys.

She tells me how first experiences shape the decisions
    we make,
are making, with boys we barely know but want to.

I think back to mine, don't divulge.
So this explains it does it?

This explains it all.

To Be Woman -

Dance sporadically.
Always in full view, silently, with nothing on.
Pick a quiet corner, in view of the dj and his decks.
Dance so wildly people dare not approach
and when they do
you are fire and brimstone,
limbs not soft enough for them to carry
limply
to their beds.

Ayesha

7 MAR, 19:28

i miss you man
i wanna chat boys,
politics & feminism with
you. not necessarily in
that order.
you good?

Blackout Poem (made from p.138 of Miranda July's
No One Belongs Here More Than You)

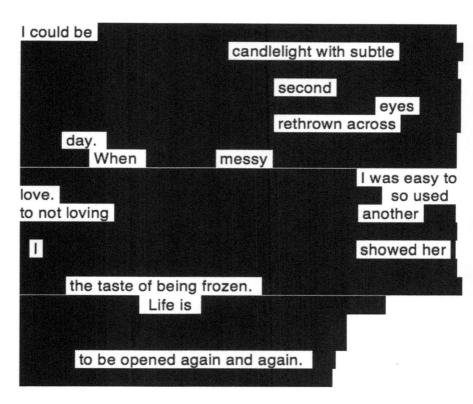

I could be

candlelight with subtle

second

eyes

rethrown across

day.

When   messy

I was easy to

love.   so used

to not loving   another

I

showed her

the taste of being frozen.

Life is

to be opened again and again.

Bed Time

In his bed,
      terms are his.

I feel in control
      with my
         skinny jeans
        against my
             skin,
top tucked in,
high heeled boots
                on.

I take off the jeans.
I still know, in the pit of my bones,
that I am safe.

But I do not feel in control.

Opal Earrings, Azure Eyes, Ocean Dress

I only came tonight to see you.
I only came tonight to see you
                              and tell you
I never loved you.
I only came tonight so you would see how good I look   ·
in blue
          and ache.

Slow, the becoming.

Slow, this becoming.
Quick to think of what we did not do,
of who we did not hold.
You say that's nature, the way it turns
and twists in unexpected ways.
I say, I heard her roar last night,
from the depths of some long feud with herself.
Nature makes oak gnarl
as it grows toward a sun
that gives too much of its light to other parts.
It always comes back, low in the sky,
proclaiming I am loving you too;
but it is not enough for oak,
who longs for sun most in night,
where she is not near or warm.

Twist of what fate, roll of which die?
We are brought here by the things we did,
but more often, by the things we did not do.
Would you agree?
We are growing skyward, still.
Slow, this expanse of land inside ourselves
that we attempt to conquer daily,
this washing away of homes we built
by the water that never promised to be pure.
We have stayed up to listen to the rattle of our hearts
once all the trains have passed.
This body of mine is a window
I have not got around to double glazing,
it shakes most when the wind taps like it has forgotten
its keys and wants to get back in.
Sometimes I am the wind outside my own body,
find myself tapping on my hip bone, or chest,
not remembering how I got outside,
or why I closed the door behind me.

SABRINA MAHFOUZ

Sabrina Mahfouz was raised in London and Cairo. Her work includes the plays *Chef*, *With a Little Bit of Luck*, *Clean*, *Battleface* and *the love i feel is red*; the poetry collection *How You Might Know Me*; the literary anthology *The Things I Would Tell You: British Muslim Women Write* and the BBC shows *Breaking the Code, Railway Nation: A Journey In Verse* and *We Are Here*. She received a Fringe First Award for *Chef* and won a Sky Arts Academy Poetry Award.

Boats in a Storm

In response to Bakhuizen

ART UK Film

Look.
How does a painting capture
stillness in chaos?
Is it through the narrow range of grey
the refusal to smudge edges?
Or is it that in the wild but contrived waves
of a painted storm belongs our true future?
Frothy, merciless, cold –
we are seized.

There sit 287 people in Parliament
who'd replace humanity's complexity
with clear and simplified blocks of colour,
make children the distant background of a painting,
matt polish pushing salvageable suffering from sight.
They would have us nod in front of oil on canvas,
I agree, it's an extraordinary depiction
of a terrifying moment.
Applaud us to retreat into a disorder without detail,
the patient artifice of babels
bodies that are hardboiled,
awaiting the peeling.

Look.
A sun and steeple in the distance –
does the artist suggest we can be saved
from cauldron clouds and augmented oceans?
I think that will require more than sun and steeples,
more than ropes flung to shore,
more than sculptured outlines of what is 'right'.
It will require, simply, all of the people
to steady our boats in a storm.

Admitting you are an addict (tali)

That day
was too dry
for the man
paying in drugs
to enter me.

My mouth too
quarried chalk valley
tunnel dust fall
saliva for fingers
to add lubrication
not be possible.

He, disgusted, pulled
I, desperate, pushed
squeaking, onto him
climbing rope, chafe.

Could not let
little liquid lack
ruin this deal.
I soldiered on
sandpaper onion salt
transform mud prints
pant real happiness.

He was able
to get
where I needed
him to get
to get
what I needed.

Good Woman

You tell me I'm a good woman
and I think
I've known many good women.

They've sprung from mattresses
when gravel has rained through the window
scratching the glass of the bedside clock.
They've taken their clothes off
to dress another's wound
haven't put them on again unless it healed.
They've swilled words in their mouths
until tumours have triumphed
and still, they never spat.
They've cleaned the arms of old men
who only ever washed them
with belt buckled whiskey breath.
They've stolen days from the sky
so that the ground can be stronger
hold our weight for longer.
They've laid on paper in blue biro
to make the bricks seem as kickable
as the cotton wool she uses on her eyes.
They've bled tequila on dancefloors
to move better to the sound
of never being good enough.

Because they never are,
good women.
You will find them alone
in the pockets of a world
that was never tailored to fit them.
You will find them alone
at the bar where a layered blur of sorrow
comes to become.
You will find them alone
behind desks pushed against windows
that have never disturbed the air.
You will find them alone
in rooms ornamented with faces
that never come to call.
You will find them

and when you do
they will be good to you
and before you leave
you will say
you are a good woman
and she will nod
as if it is enough to be good
without being loved.

the year of two thousand sixteen in signs

(1) There's a sign

it says
HANG THE REPIST
it means

the small flame of our candle
simply melts white wax
as we walk streets
by painted temples

same as he did
when he took the child
she looking for rainbow puddles
friends to play with, no time for prayers
only just old enough to say
four years of coaxing consonants to say

I want to go home now.

Her fractured body found car park cold
family loudly told, we will find them we will.
They don't.

(2) There's a sign

it says
THEY CAN'T KILL US ALL
it means

of course they can almost
they killed almost an entire race before
erase any remaining marks on the whiteboard
never use permanent pen, you know this.
It's not beyond imagination.
What is beyond imagination?
Perhaps suffocating on chroma
desperate for air like anticipatory drone bombs
held back by button-stuck sticky donut thumbs

belonging to the land of the free:
free to what free to mock free to jail
free to hate free to name free to fire
free to rape free to hit free to rob
free free free free free free free free
what does such a word mean
when you exist on a Kill List longer than the Nile?

(3) There's a sign

it says
NO HUMAN IS ILLEGAL
it means

some people have
seen cracked clouds of boats above
skinned tails of mermaids
spoke to their babies through salt-mills
and still
they must just want nice teeth.

A girl is born to a blanket of shrapnel
little mouth wailing that she is alive
a forest dries into safety deposit boxes
grocery shops cost a year's salary
a year's salary is sludged into drainpipes
the girl full of metal cannot grow, she goes.
There is one child left now, save him, go
lonely son go and take your place amongst
theft, murder, speeding, vandalism, arson
be illegal
but be you, alive, heart beating
until I can impound you back to my arms.

(4) There's a sign

it says

JOURNALISM IS NOT A CRIME
it means

as long as we say what you want us to say,
which is nothing that you haven't already said.

Do you think words sleep scattered just for you
like culled lavender buds
lilac, fragrant, waiting?

We forge Morse codes for modernity
hoping no politician can decipher them
because to write plainly
is to compose a damp, square cell
or otherwise stab broken bulbs into our hands.

(5) There's a sign

it says
THAWRET EL GHALABA
it means

literally, Revolution of the Poor
but we all know it hasn't been that
when was it ever
even if it is their skin stretched on placards
even if it is their children who know a Frappuccino
is the same price as one month's bread
but who cares anyway
cos they met a man who said with a firm hand
you can earn two fresh Frappuccinos in one day
just don't tell anyone, especially not the General,
children should not have so much caffeine.
I mean your mother, don't tell her.

This was a lie.

There's not even a sign.

BELINDA ZHAWI

Belinda Zhawi's a Zimbabwean born writer, educator & resident of London. She's co-founder & host of the bi-monthly poetry social, BORN::FREE. Belinda was the 2016/17 Institute of Contemporary Arts Associate Poet. She's currently working on her debut pamphlet collection.

On Legalising MaryJane

You remember
your grandfather's imprecise smile
teeth a yellowing white
like the sun's glare at high noon;
lips almost black like night on a full moon.

Mornings were spent
tending to his fields
before meeting afternoon,
under the shade of the msasa
armed with a worn leather bound bible;
old newspapers &, a worn leather pouch.

Your assigned role:
grab a piece of lit firewood
from the kitchen hut for him
to light what you thought to be
 newspaper rolled cigarettes.

You remember your grandfather's eyes;
they had clouds in them,
deep and grey, the sky of a storm
brewing for hours. They never flickered
 at the first puff but that yellowing smile
would spread, as the smell lingered
like wet firewood. He'd hum to himself

like a man quietly praying,
vibrating for rain. The night he died
you had not seen him for a decade.
You sat in your mother's garden
about to smoke your first spliff,

your brother next in the broken chair
you watched him hold the thinness of the Rizla
between both forefinger and thumb,
his hands like your grandfather's.
The first puff made you cough
till your eyes streamed, brother laughed before

Relax, breathe through your mouth.

By third inhale
you'd found a new friend
in an old smell that hung over the English night.
You know what, yeah? They should legalise this shit.
I read online, it treats glaucoma y'kno.

You knew but kept silent, looked at your brother's
inherited hands & realised your grandfather
as a healer who'd puffed his way through
newspapers
to make the clouds in his eyes
rain out the bind of no longer seeing
the world

in the precise light of night and day.

Lonely Londoner,

is a daughter raised to pray at dawn but now creeps through the back door on most nights, minutes before sunrise, eyes raw and heavy; body full of smoke. She wants to shrink herself into pretty; motivated by a closetful of dresses a size smaller. She can mostly be found ten toes deep in a blue carpet, or by the window which stays half open to blow out the smell of hash. Lonely girl sleeps most days away or watches them sway to wind's howling song, in the tiny forest behind her mother's house

She likes the confluence of the forest and the houses made out of council estate concrete; as though feeding from each other. On some days this unlikely communion
gets her out of bed but on the bad ones the grey swallows the forest; there is nothing she can do to stop it. Lonely girl stays stoned, with red hungry eyes
inspects her lonely mid-section
in the mirror,
trying to become woman.

Old ticket stubs - receipts of solo dates, reminders of both mania and vitality. Maybe, even, joy! They are tacked to peeling wallpaper as though it knows that nothing lasts forever. Sometimes you can see her almost forget her mother's depression. How it hid
in leather belts; under long welts of deep blues and deep reds.

Cathedral

My body does not belong to me
like I thought it did.

My legs - concrete pillars,
anchored into the ground.

I am a red fortress
of stones tightly stacked
into each other. Head
abound with noise like rain
on corrugated iron.

They say bodies are temples,
made for worship,
adorn them with silver,
hyssop & myrrh.
Well, mine's known trespassers,

heretics, & thieves who threw fire
bombs through the windows.
Even with me lit,
licked in flames,
they still wanted to break in.

Vultures,
that picked at my eyes
down to the socket holes.
Ransacked & fled.
Left my mouth redecorated;

coated in the dry taste of salt.
Instead, I wait for the earth
to turn me all things white
& circular like a girls' club,
like secrets at school. In shape

more or less like a church.
I'm still flaming brick walls,
flagrant and blue.

Full of a heat that reminds me
  daily that my body

still does not belong to me
like I thought it did.

25

i used to be a girl
asleep & unaware
of the fire flowers under my skin

a girl asleep & unaware
of the power in the crook of a woman's smile
how dark it becomes
like the lining of a moribund firecracker

when she gets her way
before she earns it
i used to be an ancient city
fallen   &   apart
a one way ticket to hell
that could stoke fires like sin
in pot-bellied uncles of no relation

ashamed about their stares
a girl   a broken gate
asleep & unaware of her legs
how   they can   curve &   soar
breasts like two human heads
under a collarbone like timber truss
soft belly
large feet, like anchored boats

my best friend once said
smoke blowing out of her mouth
i live in this body
asleep   & unaware
that i was in combat with my own house
like my body was the fall of jericho's walls

i live in this arse larger than a country
these tree trunk thighs
intricately hennaed by stretchmarks
& oh my, has this girl stretched?

Dear Whinchat,

"The whinchat is a small perching bird... It winters in central and southern Africa." – Royal Society of the Protection of Birds

i)

I heard that,

once the first spark of a British summer starts to rise

out of the ashes of spring you like

       to fly over seas;

over mountains;

sometimes even over the odd desert storm.

Over the souks of Marrakech;

     over the cries of
     mothers

in the outskirts of Kinshasa;

     over the march of
   armed,

bare footed boys who blend themselves into dark forests

      to stay alive. Over the pulsing
          hives

      of ever-growing cities;

over the hum of generators in case of sudden power
cuts.

      `Over former colonies

that still scarred with leftover pain; over red dust roads

and broken railways.
                                        Over beaten up paths

in rolling maize fields; over the laughter

of kids playing football

                        in dusty parks. Over everything which exists

                                under the sky that covers the

                                        trail from Cairo to Cape.

ii)

It has been ten years since I left home.
                        I've forgotten how at dusk the sun slowly sinks
into the ground and the sky looks like a still blaze.

                        I've forgotten how the night spreads itself
in the folds of a light cold wind;
                        I've forgotten the sound a metal pail,

tied to thick long rope, makes when it falls
into wells swollen with a full night's rain.
                        I've forgotten the feel of an early morning

how the eastern horizon would birth the sun
till the skies turned violet as a cockerel spread
its wings wider than its wake-up crow.

                        I've forgotten my grandmother's face;
both grandfathers are now dead.
My first language's started to wilt on my tongue.

When I speak to cousins back home my mouth feels

like it's full of the water that dead leaves flail in.

                          I feel like home has forgotten me.

iii)

Uprooted from one land to be planted in another,
the cold has bitten my ears raw.
My hair's started to thin at the edges;

its deep brown colour has shrunk to a dry ash.
This cold island has serrated me down
to a rough dullness. I heard that

you prefer to sun in the mornings
of savannah winters as you study
the light chill of their breeze

press brown grass back into hard, cracked earth.
Next time when the first spark of a British summer
starts to rise out of the ashes of spring,

                    bring me along so I can stop forgetting.

SELINA NWULU

Writer, poet and Young Poet Laureate for London 2015-6. Her work is often inspired by global justice, politics and protest. She has performed across the UK at a number of venues and festivals as well as internationally, including a literary tour across north east India with the British Council. Her work has been featured on a number of websites and magazines including i-D, the Guardian and Blavity. Her first chapbook collection, *The Secrets I Let Slip* was published by Burning Eye Books in September 2015 and is a Poetry Book Society recommendation.

Before

Before illegal
Before becoming the influx, the scar, the stain
Before finding my new name in a scuffed English novel
Before Jane
Before mastering the sturdy handshake
Before never using it
Before swallowing the lilts of my own tongue
Before forcing my mouth to e-nun-ci-ate
Before being misunderstood
Before dreaming of my mother's songs
Before learning the spirals of British decorum
Before *cup of tea, anyone?*
Before yearning for a belonging I could name

Before the sound of my laugh began to decay
Before the grope of polyester
Before my prayers mocked me
Before Go Home ricocheted from mouths to vans
Before dreaming of going home
Before each footstep became an apology
Before *how destitute exactly?*
Before *not destitute enough*
Before application refused
Before temporary
Before knowing
Before the stain, the scar, the influx
Before illegal

Before

Hollow

I can understand the importance
of my mother's motherhood.

And I have watched
crowns placed upon
those who have embraced
the revered entrails of maternity,
those who have draped it in
softness and ample bosom.
I understand.

The truth is far too much
beautiful tangle
too much bruise
for the maternal platitudes
we have inherited,
I understand.

But I am yet to hear anything else
I can earn a crown for
and while I have no desire
to be kept up at night,
winded by the weight of sacrifice,
indecision can weigh just as heavy,
can cause just as many sleepless nights.

A mother can become hollow
waiting and waiting
for a second becoming,
watching her daughter running
in the opposite direction
the cycle of motherhood
disintegrating

a triumph
a tragedy

Cuppa

Put the kettle on.
I'm not being funny but he's well fit
no, you don't understand
they're all sinking in the Mediterranean sea
I'm actually speaking objectively here
our borders have become dense and long
it's more an observation really
his face is near symmetrical
and their ships have burst into splints
it's hypnotising
the sea is bloated with people's limbs
it's post attraction really
I'm appreciating him as a work of art
their memories did not make it either
well, of course I wouldn't say no!
they're all sinking in the Mediterranean sea
but that's not the point
anyway, we still going out Friday?
watch how the bubbles float and pop.
Kettle's boiled.

Two Sides of a Coin

There is a girl, who looks like me,
walking through the streets of Lagos.
She is freshly plucked mangoes and forehead beads of sweat.
She is flat shoes and a head wrap on Sundays.
She is a collision of patterns chasing each other.

She looks like me but her vowel sounds have shrunk,
there are no Yorkshire undertones here.
Instead she speaks in half songs,
rolls Igbo off her tongue like blooming hibiscus
and wears her ancestors' sayings on her chest like armour.

She weaves through this downtown scene in fluid choreography:
the joke thrown to a passing neighbour,
the pause and smell of the pile of peppers in the market.
Each act has a home in this moving composition,
you can see her belonging in the sway of her hips.

If you look closely enough,
you can see how her shoulders sigh like mine,
can hear her life in the drag of her flat feet
and feel their tendency to wander.
We both laugh with the weight and depth of a church bell.
On a good day it will throw our heads back.

Sometimes I see these two versions of myself
like two sides of a coin: heads – here, tails – over there.
I wonder why the coin landed on this side.
I wonder which version would have laughed the most.

Tough Dragons

She draws the cliffs of Llanberis and sends it to
the only person who would cry and understand.

It's morning and she can still feel the day in her hands.
The morning she stood up to her father,

she trembled, wearing a scarf from Morocco:
This place is my bones; I don't care if you don't like it.

He said:
*You are fiercely intelligent and when you figure out how
to use them, your words will slay the toughest of dragons.*

She clears her wardrobe, giving away clothes
she doesn't recognise herself in.

When

When he goes

your mouth will be an empty seabed
words will leave like weary ships
on the barren port of your tongue

When he goes

you will be jacked up on stale grief
your veins will be all hiss and grit
your face a clenched fist

When he goes

You will not use the word *hate*
(though its vowels will stick between your teeth)
you will save that word

for the pillow
for the wall
for the darkness

Encyclopaedia

He thinks me an encyclopaedia,
scrapes his fingers through the depths of my chapters
and tries to rip my binding
so he can separate and hang up my pages,
searching for proof of my sadness.
He will not stop until every line has been conquered,
will not rest till all words have been crushed into their vowels.

He thinks me an encyclopaedia
and then wonders why I have become a closed book.

Jack in a Box

After Simon Armitage

His hair is steel wool
and his eyes are metal marbles
and his stare is a rusty vice
and his nose is a used test tube
and his mouth is a drawbridge
and the gap between his teeth is a cave
and his words are bats escaping
and his tongue is a jungle
and his laugh is marbled meat
and his chin is coconut husk
and his neck is a faded oak tree
and his shoulders are weathered cliff edges
and his chest is a stained glass window
and his lungs are crushed roses
and his breath is a cobweb come winter
and his stomach is knotted rope
and his arms are ripped Bible pages
and his palms are coffee-stained atlases
and his fingers are homeless
and his legs are burning matches
and his feet are train tracks
and his shadow is blunt pencil
and his tears are chloroform
and his doubts are a lighthouse
and his intentions are two-day-old flowers
and his smile is a dusty piano

and his heart is a jack in a box,
it has not yet opened.

Be Silent

As Egypt shook, I checked the mirror for love handles,
flicked through its featured howls in a magazine,
fists punching through pixels
framed through coffee mug smears.

Newspapers gave me pictures of Palestine
folding in on itself, fleeing from love lost.
Crumpled civilians dodged my doodles
and idle to-do lists.

As my remote switched on Syria,
I checked my stomach in the TV's reflection,
sucked in cheek bones and imagined myself downsized,
the glare of machine guns in the background.

The world spins off its axis.
I misunderstand as I over-tweeze.
I hear my heart beat louder than theirs
until I forget even having remembered.

BRIDGET MINAMORE

Bridget Minamore is a writer from and based in south-east London. Having started writing with the National Theatre, she has been commissioned by the Royal Opera House and Historic England, performed at the Roundhouse and the Southbank Centre, and been a repeat guest on BBC Radio 4's Women's Hour. With Point Blank Poets she has performed in both Rome and Vancouver, and was shortlisted to be London's first Young Poet Laureate. In 2015 Bridget was chosen as one of The Hospital Club's Emerging Creatives, and more recently as one of Speaking Volumes' '40 Stars of Black British Literature'. She has an English degree from UCL, regularly teaches drama and poetry workshops, and is part of the creative team behind Brainchild Festival. As a journalist, Bridget has written for The Guardian, Pitchfork, The Pool, and Newsweek. Her first pamphlet of poetry *Titanic* (Out-Spoken Press) came out in May 2016.

'Frape'

I

Hard 'F'
beating down
upon my chest

disguising
the word
I hate to say
as badly as a
fingerprinted
guilty-verdict
balaclava.

II

You arrived like Wolverine
tearing through the pixels
of my computer screen,
reminding me
rocks in rivers can
refuse to be moved;

'You must remember that day'

You say

each time you stain a status update.

rape.

Rape
is a good Christian white girl
14 to 16 years of age
in a maxi dress and puffa coat
with her hair hidden away
and flat sensible shoes on
coming home from school
in the daylight
at 3 in the afternoon
walking the safe route home
past lots of people
down the high street
having called her Mum
five minutes earlier
being pulled into a dark alleyway
by a stranger she's never seen before
who is much older
and him having sex with her
using his penis and her vagina
as she fought back the whole time
screaming the word "NO"
very loudly
scratching him the whole time
collecting his DNA
calling the police straight after
giving a thorough statement
that she repeats
6 months later
in court
putting him away for 15 years.

Rape
is a 25-year-old getting ready for a night out
telling her mates she wants to sleep
with a certain friend she knows well
taking condoms in her purse
as she assumes they'll have sex
and she has condoms left over from her last conquest
the night before
wearing a short skirt and a low cut top
because she likes her body
and she wants to show it off

and high heels she can't walk in
or run away in
getting to the party
getting very drunk, very quickly
feeling sick
throwing up
continuing to drink
ignoring her friends' requests to go home early
staying out alone
seeing the guy she likes
walking up to him
going outside
kissing him
touching him
performing a sex act on him
with her mouth
finishing
going inside
drinking some more
dancing provocatively
drinking some more
passing out
waking up with no recollection of the rest of the night
apart from a few bruises
she attributes to the alcohol
feeling well enough for a couple of days
then
getting sent a photo from an old mate
of the guy from the night
doing things to her
with his hands
with her eyes closed
and a lifeless face
then
being sent another photo the next day
of the guy doing more things to her

that she can't remember because she wasn't awake
and her going to him
and him saying sorry for the pictures
and her saying but what about touching me
and him looking shocked

and him saying she said it was ok
before she passed out
and her saying but I was passed out then, the second time,
and him saying I thought you were up for it
and her saying but I was passed out
and him saying you never said "NO"
very loudly
and her saying I didn't say "YES"
or even "yes"
or even "…yes?"
which is sort of a "NO"
or a "no"
it's even sort of a "…no?"
and him looking confused
and her saying I was passed out
I was passed out
and her telling her mates
and them saying but we thought you were up for it
you told us all you were up for it
you told us all that you wanted something to happen
and her saying but I was passed out
and them saying didn't you touch him, the first time,
and her saying but I was passed out, the second time
I didn't want something to happen while I was passed out
and her telling her Mum and sister
and them saying we thought you liked him
and her saying but I was passed out
and her sister adding you didn't say no though
and her Mum adding well at least it wasn't real sex though
and her saying but I was passed out
and her going to the police
and her telling them what happened
and them telling her she could make a statement
and her telling them what happened
and the policewoman asking if she said "NO"
very loudly
and her saying I was passed out
and the policewoman nodding her head
and writing it all down
that she didn't say "NO"
very loudly
she didn't say "NO" at all

and then going to the guy's house to make a statement
and him being angry
and saying she was up for it
I've got the texts to prove it
and their friends finding out
and them being angry
and saying she was up for it
we've got the texts to prove it
and them not talking to her
at all
because she's ruining his life
she's ruining his life
and a month going by
and the police calling her up again
saying they don't have enough evidence
and don't drink so much next time
and her making it up with her friends
and seeing the guy again
and her apologising for all the trouble she caused him
and going out for drinks with him and all their friends
and never bringing it up again
but making sure she's never quite alone with him
and her Mum saying later
well at least that's over.

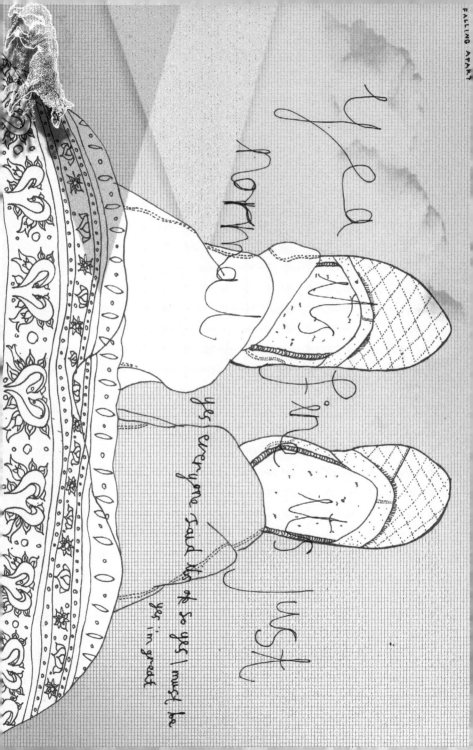

yea

normal

its fine

just

yes everyone I said it's ok so yes I must be

yes i'm great

Black James Bond

elderly, balding,
Daily Mail-buying
pink-crinkly skin-owning
non-Ian Fleming-reading
men,

their sons' mouths, stunted

stemmed by what
their fathers call
"political correctness"

opinions squirming below the surface
finally penned by eager fingertips typing

"it's just like a black Annie, unnecessary, and it takes away from the
essence of the man, it's exactly as if I cast George Clooney as Martin
Luther King, but say anything about artistic integrity and you get
called a–"

                    dancing around the word as if it was this
                    their white masculinity depended upon

For the Black Girls with White Names

I

Where do these names come from? These Catholic bastions of femininity,
almost certainly a throwback to colonialism, not weird necessarily but
odd? These Agathas, Anastasias, Mariannes, Doreens, Vivians, Ophelias,
Reginas and Robertas? These girls in flip-flopping chale-wate with shiny
brown skin, hair bound with thread and kept neat with the threat of a
peppered hand's beating: they don't look like Beryls or Ediths or Noras
Sometimes these names nestle next to English and Dutch and Portuguese
surnames that force her
liberal Western guilt beyond the surface,
let it gasp for fresh air.

Benson and Menson, Kammerling and Grant, De Souza and Da Costa,
surnames displayed like badges of honour. A taxi driver or hotel chef
eagerly explaining that his surname means he must possess some
English or Dutch or Portuguese ancestry, no-one wanting to remind him
or giving a flying fuck it's a certainty that Western surname means
some poor skinny girl from Cape Coast was raped repeatedly by some
Lisbon-born soldier cunt who seemingly found the reek of a child who
hasn't washed for 7 months as she waited to be shipped to the Americas
as a field slave attractive.

II

Your Name is a weight. It sits upon your mother's shoulder, watches the
teasing her nieces get each lunchtime when Ryan Quinn's older brother
says Abena and Akua sound like nigger fruits, tells her she chose wisely.
Your Name is a lake surrounded by land that does not belong to you, and
Your Name is loose, it droops and falls and hangs off of you, keeping itself
slack. Your name is a noose, perhaps. Weighted by its own cliché, wrapped
around your neck, and Your Name is a ruse. It lies about the truth of your
Catholic convert grandmother and the way she calls herself Englishwoman
whilst you feel you cannot.

Your Name is not yours it is theirs you feel, and it cuts into the skin
at the base of your back. Your parents, they took this shiny pink thing,
this ready-made covering that blurs your brown skin on white paper and
through phone lines so your White Name and your White Voice caresses
eyes and ears that your Dark Skin would slap. They draped you in it, this
heavy choking British-born noun, this watery oversized battleground,
this no-man's land between a pool of large red herrings to help you fit in,
and the smiling midwife telling your mother she was mispronouncing
her daughter's first name.

Nana

Cleaning the flat with the same vigour
Your last breath must have had

Shaking the dust I don't normally notice;
Mum always does

Stoic, your seventh-born sits in the sitting room
Today she doesn't care about much, but

My eyes have become razor lights
Slicing with every blink

Cutting through darkness
I sweep the stirred mites up

Preparing for our visitors –
Soon, the Aunties will come

Husbands carrying crates
To pay for the next 8 hours

       Distracting myself beforehand
       I wipe the flat from top to toe

       Knowing they will compliment
       This final show of respect

-

Welcome, welcome
       Please, take a seat
A prayer to begin
       We sing our grief in Ghana
            Voices clutching sympathy
Songs burdened by God
       Music makes words lighter
The lament ends –

               Can I get you a drink Auntie?

-

I am too hot in my parents' living room

Relatives, friends and casual acquaintances
Stoke the fire with imported bottles

West African Guinness adds fuel to the flames

In the early hours of the morning
Brown glass stacked at our feet
We will have made a pyre to put you on

Volumes

Your country is a hand grenade
My country was its pin

The family you left behind
The hand the grenade's in

Your children are fishing hooks
Cast out before you

Your children are armbands
They float if they can

Your face is a thumbprint
You all look alike

A boatful of blurred lines
A mass of dark dots

You are staining my free newspaper
Blurring the font and obscuring the print

Handing yourselves in
To a place that doesn't want you

JOELLE TAYLOR

Queen of spoken word and an out-spoken feminist, her last collection was published by Burning Eye in 2014, and she's set to release a new collection with Out-Spoken Press. She curates and hosts Mother Foucault, and was awarded a Fellowship of the Royal Society Arts in 2015 as well as being named as one of Southbank Centre's Nelson Mandela Change Makers for positively affecting cultural Britain. She has been co-ordinating SLAMbassadors UK since 2001 and her support and enthusiasm for this project has been immense.

Songs My Enemy Taught Me

(I)

Silence was a song my enemy taught me.

I carry the war in my womb.

At night it kicks
and sings stories of the
first night that war came calling.

Blackpool.

1973.

Small. We are refugees of the economic crisis that has cut power lines
and muted the mouths of coal mines and left Uroborus dole queues
flailing in its wake.

The seaside hotel flung open its doors for us, and flapped its window
sashes, as we arrived to make camp for the winter. Songs were written
about us.
We pitched our tents in the living room. It was Christmas. Strangers'
ballroom danced around us.

At midnight we dug ourselves into our muddy beds. Everybody slept.
I stayed on watch. I am still on watch.
When the war came I was eating vol-au-vents from a paper plate.
When the war came I was forcing my Cindy doll into a shapeless Eagle
Eye action man uniform. When the war came I was Sellotaping a rifle
to the frozen hand of my Barbie.

When the war came it was gentle. When the war came it was singing.
The scent of war is Old Spice, is lager, is late night take away. The
sound of war is silence. Is a small girl with a mouth as wide as a coal
mine that eats the whole town.

In the morning there were boot marks across the board games.

(II)

The bed is cold and my teeth are abandoned buildings
and somewhere there is the smell of something burning.

A book. A flag. A letter.

In my room at the top of the seaside hotel
there is a single bed with a white sheet.
I cannot think of anything to write on it.

The bed is a slowly developing photograph:

Here's everyone around the dinner table.
They are smiling like carved meat.
No one notices that the daughter is eating herself.

Here's you walking home from school.
Your shadow walks behind you as if ashamed.
Even the trees whisper about you.
You have embarrassed the wind.

Here's him. And him. And him.
A family portrait. Successful. Ironing their uniforms
and double-folding their smiles
Catching children delivered
from the conveyor belt of their wives wombs
and holding them up to the bare light bulb to bless.
It's okay. They are boys.

Here are the stairs
And here, the long corridor you are afraid to walk along
Perhaps it is your cervix.
It is your cervix.

(III)

My womb is a war zone after everything is taken.
After the soldiers have left
spitting into the palms of their hands,
after the shelves have been emptied and only sell nothing,
after the nothing gathers in great mountains

at the sides of the streets,
after the streets are running with hungry ghosts,
after women's skins are slung from washing lines,
after children write their names in the dust
that was once that of their fathers.

--

I carry the war in my womb.
Perhaps this is what happened:
Someone said my hymen was a door
behind which rebels were making plans
and they kicked it in
paced the room and filled their pockets with valuables:
My mother's wedding ring. My first tooth.
A bright blue hair bobble. Your address. This.
They wanted to know where I was hidden.
I wanted to know where I was hidden.
I am the corner of the room.
I am a crime scene.
An invaded land.
An oil-rich country.
I will be divided equally between nations.

(IV)

12 years old.

There are small bodies washed up
on the shores of my eyes.
When my photograph is taken
another girl's face appears instead of mine.

(V)

There are men seated quietly
at municipal Formica desks
at the neck of my womb.

You do not look like your photograph they say
please state the purpose of your visit.

Did you pack these bags yourself?

My sandbag hips.
My barbed wire hill.
Many will die defending it,
others will drown in the sediment of a trench
whose walls are always caving in.

My cunt is a bomb crater the villagers gather around the edge of
and peer into. Sometimes smoke rises from deep within. These are
my ghosts.

These are messages in a lost language. Capture them in jars. Display
them on suburban mantelpieces. In memes. On T-shirts. Smile. Be
my friendly enemy.

(VI)

When you are impregnated by war
you give birth to bullets.
Name them. Show them his scent.

The palm of my small right hand is a creased map
to safety. I am stopped at the border.
I cannot remember my name in your language.

My skin is a white flag

I am waving it now. I am holding my skin above my head.

Stop shooting. Stop shooting. Stop shouting.
War is an unexploded kiss, buried. The battle ground
is the bedroom in which two people stand
in opposing trenches behind sandbag pillows

saying *I Love You* wrong. That's not how you say it.
This is how you say it.

--

My skin is partitioned.
This bit is yours.
Parts of my body speak different languages;

after the war I was colonised.
Use my blood to power your generators,

dig deep in me for your gemstones,
harvest my hair and eyelashes, these
drips of words on my chin.
And you:
You I give my womb to.
Feed it well. Walk it when needed.
Listen at night to its curling song.

(VII)

the girl whose eyes are shallow graves beneath suburban patios goes
to school and rows of heavy wooden lidded desks are filled with the
smiling dead. When the world ended nobody noticed. The sun has
eaten itself. Skeleton birds mutter bone songs.

Her mother and father tell jokes about her.
Everybody laughs.
The girls whose eyes are fox holes laughs.
The teacher laughs.
Children gathered like litter around the stairwell laugh.
The social worker laughs.
The policeman man laughs.
The doctor laughs.
The psychiatrist giggles.

The world ends.

(VIII)

I remember how silence was a choir.
There's you in the kitchen, vibrato.
There's you at the back of the class, soprano.
There's you walking home, tenor.

Your solo silences are everywhere.

(IX)

This is not what I meant to say.
I once witnessed my own murder. It was Wednesday.
It is always Wednesday.

After my death people continued talking to me
as though I were still there.

After my death people tried to hold me
but their hands passed through my skin.
After my death I came back to haunt myself,
often catching glimpses of my ghost
sitting in the same chair as me, speaking
through my mouth, ahead of me
in the dinner queue, my bright blue bobble
dancing just out of reach in a crowd,
an ankle disappearing around a corner.

(X)

When war was teething, it rubbed its soft gums against pavements
and trees and wallpaper and lovers. It refused to let go of my hand in
public. I lost sight of war once in the park and its screams were sirens
and the wail of bombs. I hit people I love: my bombing is imprecise.
This is common. This is to be expected.

(XI)

in the hospital she lies in bed –
she has always lied in bed –
They ask her questions and she focuses
on the spelling of the answers
She is afraid she will not get them right.
She cannot get them right.
The true answer is the wrong answer.

(XII)

They show her children who do want to die.
They are friendly. One offers food
that she knows will eat her.

She is shown a photograph of an ugly overdose.
She is shown obituaries etched in fingernails.

In his pockets,
the man with the papercut mouth has a box.
It too is small. It too is velvet.

Inside the box, mounted at the centre, is a large tear, collected a
drip at a time
from all of the children under his care.

Tears are crystal balls.

If you look closely at it, you can see your future, he says.
She leans close.

She sees nothing.

(XIII)

When the talking begins the villagers hide in cellars or run in the shade of trees to the other side of the hill. The girl with the dugout eyes watches them leave and stops speaking. She talks to a piece of paper in her hand instead. People queue up to look at it. There are so many peering over her shoulder that she has to stand on the hill and read it out to everyone. They clap. They look pleased. She forgets what she is saying.

(XIV)

For Christmas I give my mother an uncomfortable truth.
She wears it when I visit.
(XV)

At the core of every woman is the womb.

The bright angry pearl formed of grit and lies and courage and
unreturned phone calls and regret
rubbed for centuries against one another.

They come to prise it out.
It is a summer morning.
When she awakens she is surrounded by strangers
stranded on islands of tight white beds –
archipelagos strewn across the ward.

She waves
but every stranded woman
is waving to someone else
who is waving to someone else.

Ships pass and do not see them.

(XVI)

Later I am dressed in bunting and songs are composed to keep my spirits up. Later we are given ration books of kisses, three hand-holdings a month. One dry night. There is never enough to go around.

Grown men on street corners cower and wonder at the cracks cobwebbing their faces, not knowing they are smiles.

(XVII)

After the war there was singing. After the war there were ceremonies of remembrance. We remember the living, and finally carve our own names into our gravestone teeth.

After the war we set out to find the others and guide them home. We lit fires in our windows and tapped Morse over screwed rubble. Some rubble tapped back.

Some rubble grew hands and we pulled on them until we had uprooted a forest of women, shaking their heads of soil, of shame, and brushing silence from their shoulders. Thank you, they said. Thank you.

We have been waiting.

RACHEL LONG

Poet, facilitator and literary events curator. Shortlisted for Young Poet Laureate for London in 2014. She is alumna of the Jerwood/Arvon Mentorship Scheme (2015-16), and leads Octavia, Poetry Workshops for Women of Colour at Southbank Centre.

The Girl Who Could Do The Most Sit Ups

She shows me the scars
careening the stomach
that won her the P.E prize, Year: 9.
I was jealous. As I am now
on walk-of-shame Sundays
of her husband and babies,
sitting round their table,
passing glazed carrots and smiling.

Tiff yanks her first maternity blouse up,
'Still jealous of these?'
Her once-lovely 32Cs, now huge, sad moons – translucent and
'only whacked out for him in the dark.'
We laugh, a little green-tinged chorus.
We want swapsies to be currency again.

My phone rings: the fuck buddy. I tell him
I'm leaving 'now, yes, I'll be with you soon.'
Her: 'Tell me where you're going tonight.'
Me: 'Nowhere we haven't been.'
She cackles, then pleads.

I map our night across her stomach,
draw a cinema, a noisy bar - dark
so I colour it in. She closes her eyes.
I walk across the bone of her bra
to the door of his flat. My finger-foot hovers
for a stretch of unmarked skin
while he fiddles for his keys.
Inside,
I tip-toe down uncarpeted stairs
- her ribs, right down to the last step,
her hip,
where they both, always,
twist out of my reach.

His Bottom Lip

Clitoral, like finding
a small, hidden part
of myself in someone else.
Nerve-wet, fleshy
- for a white guy, and stained
between life-lines with red wine
gone black.
Only this I point
with sharpest teeth.
He weighs this up. Eyes roll
over what this means,
how and where it can lead, all the things
it limits. I think this is his first time
knowing what it is to be betrayed
by a part of his own body.
Lucky.
No other part? He starts, Not even –
Be strict. *Only this.*

Kiss Me

Jut the crust-arrow of an elbow to his lips
Peel back frenulum, expose pincher-roots
of front teeth. Look
like a slave inspected on a block
Give him the middle finger sprouting two hairs
Chewing gum mole spat between breasts
Cave of prickly armpit, taste the chalk
of my deodorant. Grab of back-fat,
hear it gasp unclasped from bra. Belly
Tongue-crawl across its trenched field
Dirt scar on ankle - all around, the whole ring,
hear my mother as you do it, 'You didn't wash the bath!'
Bolt-like bunion on big toe
Split earlobe
Double chin when laughing
Cartilage between breathing
Smallest finger, underneath the nail, yes, down,
taste the poison in polish, the garlic I massaged
two nights ago into the chicken.

Sandwiches

Tiff's pressing me against school railings,
doing my eyeliner. This is how we meet proper.
I whisper in class, 'Your eyes.
Can you make mine like that?'
Like graphic novel knives.

Break-time:
against make-up rules and railings – the wire diamonds
we chat with our fingers inside. We want
engagement rings this big, so big
we can see freedom on the other side.

Her weight against me is solid and soft, a bomb
before, then after, it goes off. A weight inclusive
of the glitter on her lids, the oil spill on her lips,
the sandwiches padding her bra. Yes, the sandwiches; unbuttered,
no filling
- this is their purpose, not privilege.

See, by now, the boys know the difference
between tissue and tit, a sock and a tit,
but not yet a tit and a slice of bread.
Tiff's so smart
my new eyes weep.

Patterns

I wore Speed Dial lips, starved into a new dress,
and walked into a party last Sunday in the hope
you'd walk into the party
starving to see me.
You didn't. Still didn't. Not even peckish
for me. It was the end, and I was drunk
in a semi-circle of four men.
I left with one of them. You know him. Well,
I wanted to tell you this before he did.
If it's any shot of whisky, the whole time I turned over
the results of a spelling test. Until thirteen,
I thought stars
gathered in consolations.

JASMINE COORAY

Poet and therapist from London. Spurred by a silent adolescence, she now designs and implements a variety of projects that cultivate emotional literacy through poetry. In 2013 she was Writer in Residence at the National University of Singapore and has just finished tenure as a BBC Performing Arts Fellow with Spread the Word. Her first full collection is almost complete, and she is working on a collaborative poetry and aerial arts show with Upswing about what it means to trust. To balance her frequent reclusiveness, she does an excellent line in hugs.

Father, Phantom

She confesses she saw a light above
your favourite chair – a small blurry orb,
hovering. Quick to sweep herself up
with *probably just seeing things,*

she scrubs hard at her bifocals, blinks
as if waking from sleep. Moments on,
wet eyes and whisper betray wonder:
I felt like all the weight had been lifted.

It had to be you. Holding up was what you
did in our house: the world rested
on your beams so we could play safely
beneath, like toddlers under a dining table.

Mum's shoulders have bowed a touch;
her body, a chair with too heavy a sitter.
Your little sun exposed a rare glimpse
of how tiring she finds this heavy thing.

Quiet Men

For solace, you nestle in broadsheets,
dank sheds of home-brewed ale,
on allotments, thick fingers raking soil,

or surface to dispel a pub brawl
with a palm on the shoulder,
your eyes like expert reins.

We, your wives and sisters,
huff and groan at your muteness,
batter your ears with our noise

but silence is something you walk,
yogic on its hot coals, your
breath slow through all that stings.

We flood our senses to avert
its heat, but you've walked
that narrow strip all our lives.

From one edge to another
we walk across with you,
learning to tread without fear.

On the ugly use of the word Pussy

How terrible, to be called a soft place, a tender place,
to pulse and undulate, a sea anemone, shades of coral,
raspberry, ochre, slate, inverted guiro, bundle of nerves,

little bell ringing through the body. Stingray wings,
petal drapes, sometimes papery, and the furry cape:
thicket, landing strip, or long-whiskered samurai
     master.

We don't like to show off the features - self cleaning
pleasure zone, pink walls elastic as a cobra's throat,
a bay to take in that swimming lottery and deliver

a jackpot of new life – but you do keep giving us
this bad review, that word intoned like a machete.
How anxiously it hacks at that slippery navel cord!

It must haunt you like a ball and chain yet so many
of you spend your lives making your way back here,
by any means possible, wanting to name us your own.

Incantatum Politicus

The year candles were bought from occult shops
where glowing staff who seemed not to walk but glide,

velvet-skirted and jingling from counter to shelf, a
    rickety
cardboard temple was built, sticky with melted wax.

Here prayers were whispered to five elements,
pentagrams swung to ward against heartbreak,

acne, the bully in the school canteen. The bedroom door
leaked Nag Champa fog, and a ring binder, stripped

of French verbs, overflowed with spells - web print-outs,
the characteristic purple font holding all the magic

a fledgeling witch might need. Once I found the folder
missing, and downstairs, my mother's finger poised

on one page, the other hand brandishing a black candle,
her eyes wild, triumphant as a gold-hunter, proclaiming

I'm going to cast a spell on that arsehole Tony Blair!
Two million marched that summer against the Iraq War

and at home this woman, godless since convent nuns
caned all the worship from her, muttered incantations

over a newspaper photo, the Prime Minister's toothy
    grin
splodged with wax. Though not convinced he would
    seize

suddenly in his sleep, wake with scales or webbed feet,
here she was, clutching ritual, acting out the movements

as a child, making a sword of a stick, for a second
imagines anything to be possible, however small she
    feels.

Birds of Paradise

Steve-o fights the sound system with a series
of jokes to no one, winks when he catches

an eye. See, she liked that one! He caws,
re-twisting his crest of wilting gelled spikes.

Dylan corners a blonde on her way to the loo,
bops, side to side, protein-shake biceps flexed,

hips thrusting back and forth, fertility goods
straining against his bright brass zipper,

but Jamie has the best nest lining. At least
that's what he'd like you to think, gold watch

glinting under the passing mirrorball spots,
photographs of a cherubim nephew on cue

to soften your eyes, stir the womb. He'll score,
kiss her pretty neck too hard in a damp corner

which is more than can be said for Seamus
in his star sunglasses, pink nylon frill shirt,

glacé cherry glistening between nicotine teeth.
He mimes reeling them in on a fishing line

across the club, though the floor jolts and parts
like a shoal. A disco lothario, still mateless

at closing time, he doesn't falter at the gradual
trickle of couples, close, stumbling streetward.

The night is young! he slurs, elbow sliding off
the bar, twirling the bouncer on the way out.

SOPHIE FENELLA

Sophie is a writer and performance artist originally from London, currently based in Berlin. She can often be found performing in both the UK and and her poems have been published online and in magazines such as The Rialto, Magma, Popshot, The Morning Star and on the The Poetry School website. When she is not writing or performing she is teaching English and drama to ESL learners, and children with learning disabilities.

First Flight

Teach me how to smash music videos,
girls in the rain howling for shiny men.

Show me how to kiss her under street lamps,
waiting for buses, hands in pockets.

If flying means no more nervous laugh,
no more hidden knickers,

let feathers furl between my shoulders,
teach me the touch of the sky.

Let me catch sweat from her forehead,
make a wish on her tussled hair,

let me love my own.
See the light on her shoulder freckles,

that is worth flying for;
an end to straight forward passion,
the epicentre of tangled sheets.

After the disco

I run my hands over my hips
trying to remember:

skin is cling film
stretched over chicken carcass,
keep stretching,
keep stretching.

In case of tears:
roll shoulders back,
tuck belly button in,
keep tidy girls,
keep tidy.

Every song asks us to:
slick hips, clinch waists,
flick hair, flick hair,
punch stomach in.

Every song asks us to:
lick our lips, flex our chests,
dose ourselves in blusher
and set ourselves on fire.

I watch T.V, to distract,
she turns up on my screen
all collar bones and legs,
I turn the sound off
and watch her hip bones
reflect the sun.

Night Running

I run from the night
but find
it is in my bones,
and cannot shake the fear
of not being alone,

and shake keys in my fist
to stop
the fox screaming
from being anything
other than a fox screaming-

remembering my mother
teaching me
not to wear short skirts
around certain men –

and I pretend
to forget the sight of her
pulling her dressing gown
across her chest,

and I can't hear
falling,
and I can't see
knees buckling,

and I can't stand the night,
and I can't remember
the wet slip of darkness
following me.

Mother, I'm sorry,
worry lines never escape
the interiority of my mind,
I promise.

Girls

I've known some crazy girls in my time.

Girls who strut through toilets with knives for hands,
cutting excess meat, smearing beach coloured skin
across their chest.

Girls who spit fire at their reflection,

No, no, that's not me,
can't be me.

Girls who run through five in the morning parks,
wishing their legs were as crisp as grass,
screaming at the sky, and swearing
every bead of sweat is a medal.

Girls who drink with mouths mouthing no,
holding their hair back , getting to know
the pattern concrete makes on knee caps,
and all the while they keep singing,

No, no that's not me,
can't be me.

Girls who write dreams in lists,
1.   Let my thighs be twiggy.
2.   Let my stomach flatten.
3.   Let me melt like plastic.
Girls who won't tell jokes,
won't dance, won't run,
won't unfurl their arms
from their chests.

Girls who wear crazy
stitched from century old patterns,
only to rip the seams, to be undone.

Meat

13

Slick brown strands stuck
to my cheeks, lined my lips
with Pantene mouse. Teeth
only came out at night.

15

I wallpapered my bedroom walls
with the front cover of Vogue,
fell asleep beneath a canvas
of collarbones.

17

I earned cool points
in the toilets, when I swore
I wouldn't see the other side
of eighteen.

19

Chronic gastroenteritis
earned me a chorus of
'looking wells'.
The changing rooms
never felt so good.

21

My hands were butchers,
cutting meat in the mirror.
My knees understood the way
a bathroom floor feels.
My mouth dreamt of aborting
the food baby.

23

A friend and I shared spaghetti
for five hours, chasing food particles,
with our tongues.

25

A fifteen-year-old girls says
I'm taking up too much space.
She is holding a pair of pliers,
to widen the gap
between my thighs.

27

Hollow-eyed mannequins don't like
the kebab I eat at bus stops,
they want to smooth my stomach.
I admire their twig-like arms,
and wonder when femininity
became another word for sickness.

Liquid Diet

I gave up chocolate when the sun
cut the sleeves off your t-shirt –
eighties rock star –
now we lament chapped lips,
and I haven't touched sweets
since scales became ground teeth.

When you offered me lemonade
the glass was an abscess in my gut.
I couldn't stop noticing
grains of sugar, swirling in twisters
like a little apocalypse.

You bought me a bikini;
I said I was scared of the beach.
You don't know this, but
I fall asleep holding the sun
between my finger and thumb,

holding on to cold beer on dry grass,
holding on to yellow light dancing
on white sheets kicked in a knot
at the end of the bed.

Holding on to mornings
when my stomach feels flat,
as a midnight black sheet
engulfs the afternoon,

and I stand, shivering,
wondering how a day
could be so you.

The Desire to Escape is Human

You left my hand
next to the ash tray
I bought in Berlin,
I liked the ash stains,
marks of another life,
and the orange glass
smelt of old.

You never used it,
preferring a beer can,
or the floor, on bad days.

You cut my hand off
when my nose bled
and said I shouldn't
be so vacant, waking
is better than sleeping,
my fingers twitched
holding on to nothing.

Castaway

On Brighton beach the Pier cheers; as he shovels chalk dust into his snout, white streams drip out his nose. His eyes harden like drying glass as the powder sets in. A crew of girls catch his punch lines with their tongues; his cheeks turn grey from all the nothing. Breathing in and out, with the tide, he presses his fingers in his ears. The sea offers him silence. With the strength of a new born child, he throws his phone into the ocean, says he's had enough. I slip my fingers through his to remind him I am there. A man groans in the shadows as if to say, not like this mate, not like this, pressing his face in pebbles, hiding from what came next, his lip breaks open, beating his fists against his head he tells me not to watch. I don't want them to hear me. I pull his head into my chest and whisper; I will be your sound proof. The Pier keeps cheering, I guess it can't hear him cry, I don't know how to be a man. In the morning, when our tongues feel like sand, he says he remembers nothing.

Word Skin

I spoke French to the bus driver
after school. I was never able
to use a dictionary,
but liked to glide my eyes over

Les Liaisons Dangereuses,
admiring the shape of the letters
as one enjoys oil paints
swirling on canvas, making love
with each other.

Reading French was less dizzying
than *Hamlet,* whose pages sent me
into a state of flickering, akin
to a supermarket checkout
scanning barcodes.

In French I could unzip,
stretch my tongue, unfurl
my Peacock feathers,
swish my tail,
mutter melting butter
as the bus stopped at
Stamford Hill.

ESTHER POYER

Poet, storyteller and life coach from London, she often writes about Caribbean immigration and an imagined past from a rich Guyanese legacy, alongside the imagery and language of Black British women. She has performed poetry and live literature in the UK and as far flung as Nairobi, Kenya and she has been writer in residence for The London Design Festival at the Victoria and Albert Museum where she has facilitated art installation seminars. Overtime she began to notice the synergy between creative writing and coaching, and she has collaborated with local councils and business development agencies delivering career and business programmes for adults and young people.

English Patois

*I had roast pork for Sunday dinner, pronouncing it
'poke,' I could very well have been a sinner.*

I'd go, *poke*
and they'd all laugh
on the benches by the tennis courts,
at St Ursula's Convent School for Girls.

She'd go, *say it again!*
Amanda Goodhew
with her hair all blond, cut into a wedge
and I'd go, *poke?*

Stressing the obvious, feeling exotic
and a little bit mysterious.

They'd all laugh, this girl scrum of long hair,
pig and ponytails. The kind that responded
to a very light breeze or even the very slightest
movement of a head. Thrown back in this case,
curve of a question mark in each creamy white neck.

Why'd you say it like that?

I gestured with my palms upturned,
What like po-ak? As I tried to change it up,
say it different from my Guyanese mum and dad

as different as growing up with sun so hot
white blond rays on mud heads,
as different from the low line mist and fog
as I skipped, an apparition upon pavements.

Poke I'd go, listening (to myself) for the joke
the raisin in the rice pudding on the bench,
in the shadow of the courts. *Roast chicken,*

I laboured, *roast lamb* and —
Ohhhh! She said. *You mean roast pork!*

Red June 1976

The sun is a swatch of yellow and platinum rays,
stretching its heat through June to September.

Red June and schools out, I am so young I still sing
knick-knack paddy whack; five, six, pick up sticks –
with big brother and my baby sister. Three lion cubs
born under sun signs the centre of my universe.

The sun spills white gold glowing like treasure,
at the hem of our velvet drapes.

Boy Simba drops one leg from the top bunk,
we follow suit in night dresses that transform
Kefira girls to morning's princesses.
Cornmeal porridge, barley tea, sweet bakes
and warm milk. Hong Kong Phooey,
Button Moon and Tom 'n Jerry.

A dusty brown afro with deep side parting
for style. I drag a hairbrush across the surface
pure pleasure unclamped from my mother's knees.
From hands that score partings, oil scalps
and fingers that cornrow from temple to nape.

The sun is a Jackson Five disco beat, playing
over waves of urban greenery.

I hold my sister's sticky hand as we pad along
to Mountfield Park. Simba boy steps stealthily
on the pavement kerb. No cars bumper to bumper
the road is a long gap-toothed smile.

As the day pans out in a safari through play,
swings swing, roundabouts spin and I sing,
See-saw Marjorie Daw, with my sister riding
up then down until she falls and busts her lip
blood on teeth, there's tears and hugs.

The sun is honey as evening starts its settling in,
we're bumble bees we follow our noses home.

Sister Powell will come in the morning
for Sunday school and we'll travel in best dress
on board her chariot to Father God.

Three pairs of legs (paws in shoes), dangling from
laden pews. My brother will tug at his elasticated tie,
my sister's eyes wide as grown ups talk in tongues;
shake, rattle, roll and hit the deck, body-checked
by the Holy Spirit. I'll go home hymn singing,
There'll be light, there'll be light,
there'll be light at the river when we cross.

The sun is a silver coin in a cloud white sky,
red June cools to autumn.

A Poem about Lentil Soup and a Little Boy

In the blond hue of kitchen light
on that window spot of hers,
slicing onions draws prideful tears
shed on his first day of school.

Fresh brackets of onion make shreee,
chitter in smoky olive oil. Heirloom
saucepan's loose fitting lid, seen all
ingredients known to womankind.

Taste plentiful, rich in subtle influence.
Potato peeling layer by layer to fleshy
essence of sustenance, as raising a child
strips bare vanity and youth's foolish fare.

Rinsed lentils, flat and pinkish, removed
of bad seed. Seasoned (veggie) minced
meat well browned to tasty. Salt and pepper,
rough with the smooth. A thumbnail of sugar,

the left touch of saccharine smiles. Fills pot
with hot vegetable stock to simmer. Our lives
empty out as theirs will fulfil. Steam rises,
a flung cotton sheet, a halo over infant heads.

Soft dumpling dough rolls warm between
palms, nurtured new-born in cradled arms.
Sprinkles in narrow strands pasta vermicelli
that rise and swell as in life.

Like a Shield

After Grace Nichols

In Guyana
I get this sense
of my mother's childhood.
Loose smile, squint eyes,
adventure a fire ball in her belly.
Campbellville Housing Scheme, she'd said
in a vapour puff of chilly London air.

I need this link

this completing circle
to home,
spinning my umbrella
like a shield
against the heat.

The Menstrual World

1.
End times are new beginnings
orange, the new black of lost liberation.
Dreams tied to the earth are old desires,
falling like the great walls. The tongue,
the perfect taste and tendency to babble solutions,
while hungry infants wash up lifeless.
Television news bleeds onto living room floors
and through screens on our laptops.
We pretend that space and time have form
and turn away from the force of an invisible blow,
when end times are new beginnings.

2.
I am an indigo child, true, wild and beautiful,
dreams are made in minds and buried only by lies.
Where peace resides I slip and glide
skipping the slits of praying eyes,
never unbound since the stakes burned and
our sisters became tears stored in our throats.
There is a shift that happens within
these external manifestations that are
simple to grasp but hard to let go.
The collective knowing is the breast
releasing the finery of the heart,
as the womb persists to birth our world.

The Sky

It's only one sky, but this sky felt different —

Black to nearly blue
like,
sun soaked melanin.

One incandescent sprite
blinking among many
and the Gods, peace pipe smoking.

Tropic insects chorus a twilight

symphony, as home birds settle

on a land of many waters,
a nation of six races, my
first time home.

George Town Girl

Fine bony hand rests on pearls
her smile is open mouthed,
tongue on the tip of life.

Hot comb straightened hair,
soft curls in balmy air,
cicada drone song welcoming

family, neighbours arriving in pairs and threes.
Couples clasping hands, gait genteel
all capture the moment, Guyana marvels
at this fresh heart girl

whose oyster world dreams
reached farther than night sky
via great Empire tales and mystery.

Voices burble, the stage band plays
to a carnival of swing dresses
in polka dots, pastels and sateen's,
that spill from her willow hips in damson layered tulle.

Wink toe stilettos dance
to mythical Ma Rainey who sung
to her muse, clasping hung vintage microphone
in smoky basements
where passive rumour, tipped hats,
red lips and curled eyelash winks,
signaled the invitation.
Ma Rainey crooned as they danced
on feet that tread rustic roads
carried hope and freedom,
blessed the graves of buried slaves.

The stage band melody
is the wave of a flock's wingspan
curling through this man she knew
His silver hair and sharp tailored suit

waltzing drifts and breezes.
They had held each other too long, carrying
as she left, a diamond through air and sea.
A lost jewel that would grow inside her,
that would suckle and with no regrets
she would nurture.

Song Notes

Is like song notes falling, is
like storm rain pon zinc roof
this man's music won't leave me.

I spy him from Bourda market
he gaffing by the barber shop
under that sun bleach awning.

I have six parcels of (five)
star apple on a cotton cloth
green ones in the basket.

Wait, is how dis woman handling me fruit
thin fingers bruising flesh and she putting back?

                I feel the red in me veins.

He got that same idle way,
the charm of an easy breeze
that made me swell.

Was like song notes settling
as daisies on grass spears,
in the Kitty house garden.

Not like now. Where a single flower
grows to stand stranded
upon this craven earth.

                A daisy and its golden heart,
                made for each other.

Our fairy tales castle,
grand with pointed turret
and windows high. Not like this,

hard rain on zinc,
ghost patting me shoulder
and all the music wash away.

Bruised purple. I had
ambled off that verandah.
Each footfall a new note,

                    from an old song sheet,
                    and all the music wash away.

Rose Water and Spice

A Guyanese couple celebrate their fiftieth wedding anniversary. Five grown up children, eight grandchildren, old friends and a neighbour – forty-four years after arriving in the UK.

Dawn sunshine stretches
pavement shadows
along my street.
A swollen belly. The
expectant slim figure of him,
tidy in postman uniform.
Her slow turn comes quick
as I lean off my broom. I wave.
Good luck I'd heard. Sweeping
make-believe dust from my
polished red front step.

Red like her proud smiling lips. Knife
cutting fancy cake. My hands sting
as we clap. They lace arms,
champagne flutes to lips
sips marking the occasion.

Calypso dancing, necks
and wrists jangle with jewellery.
Gold decorated smiles, soft haired
children among the grown-up legs

and I think of my brood long gone.
Hanging plates are stopped
cogs above the fireplace. She smiles
and admires my teardrop pearls.

In the kitchen where once, amid
sweet spice and candlelight, we shared
a friendly cuppa. Whole street a black out
of frozen pipes in the snow of '83.

Hands me a china plate. Cooked-up rice
she offers, and do I want curried goats or
soused pork. I eat the floury roti,
politely contemplating heartburn.

I'd ventured into their world after four score
years and more. Let go regrets.
Rose water perfume. Scent of spice.
I make my way across our street.

ACKNOWLEDGEMENTS

Boys and Girls by Carmina Masoliver was previously published online at Kumquat Poetry.

Made.com by Rowena Knight was first published in The Rialto, issue 83.

By Sabrina Mahfouz: *Boats in a Storm* was written in response to a painting by Bakhuizen displayed at Dulwich Picture Gallery and the 2017 voting against the Dubs Agreement to allow child refugees asylum in the UK (commissioned by Art UK). *Admitting you are an addict (from the character Tali)*, is from her collection *How You Might Know Me*, Outspoken Press, 2016. *the year two thousand and sixteen in signs* was commissioned by Writer's Centre Norwich and British Council for the International Literature Showcase.

Before, Hollow, Cuppa, Two Sides of a Coin, Tough Dragons, Encyclopedia, Jack in a Box, Our Parents' Children and Be Silent were previously published in Selina Nwulu's debut collection, *The Secrets I Let Slip*, also by Burning Eye Books.

His Bottom Lip by Rachel Long was published online in The London Magazine. *Sandwiches* was Highly Commended in The Poetry Book Society Student Competition 2014 and published online *The Girl Who Could Do The Most Sit Up*s was recorded for The Wellcome Collection's Sexology Season. Patterns was previously published in Synaethesia Magazine, 'HUSH HUSH' issue.

Rose Water and Spice and *Song Notes* by Esther Poyer were first published in Loose Muse: An Anthology of New Writing by Women, Autumn 2012

With thanks to Ideas Tap, who funded the payment of these poets through Carmina Masoliver winning The Wrap-Up Fund of £500.

Lastly, a massive thank you to Burning Eye Books for all the support in taking this anthology on board.

The following were commissioned poems:

Aisling Fahey – To be woman

Sabrina Mafouz – Good Women

Belinda Zhawi – Cathedral

Selina Nwulu – When

Bridget Minamore – 'Frape' and rape.

Joelle Taylor – the birth of war

Rachel Long – Kiss Me

Jasmine Cooray – On the ugly use of the word Pussy

Sophie Fenella – Meat

Esther Poyer – The Menstrual World

SHE GRRROWLS TEAM

CARMINA MASOLIVER

Poet and educator, and part of the Burn After Reading community, and Kid Glove collective. She has been published as part of Nasty Little Press' 'Intro' series and has performed at various festivals including Latitude, Bestival and Lovebox. She also facilitates workshops, which she has done independently, as well as alongside Ross Sutherland, Niall O'Sullivan and Michael Rosen.

ROWENA KNIGHT

Rowena Knight grew up in New Zealand and currently splits her time between Bristol and London. She studied Ancient, Medieval, and Modern History at Durham University, where she established the university's Poetry Society. Her poems have appeared in the Morning Star, Bare Fiction, Magma, and The Rialto. Her first pamphlet, All the Footprints I Left Were Red, was published with Valley Press in 2016. She tweets at @purple_feminist.

NATALIE COOPER
(Illustrations)

Natalie Cooper is a creative and cultural activist of African-Caribbean descent. She is a qualified Graphic Designer and was awarded a Masters Degree in Anthropology and Sociology from SOAS, where she focused on Afro-Caribbean diaspora and religion. Natalie runs her social enterprise 'African Musical instruments' named after her illustrated educational book of the same name and works at the National Theatre in Arts Education for young people. She loves gardening, black/African history, stargazing, nature, jewellery and dancing.

MATTHEW DICKINSON
(Cover art)

Matthew Dickerson is an illustrator, graphic designer and concept artist. He has been involved in the production of flyers since the beginning and is the designer of the *She Grrrowls* website. He held his first solo exhibition in 2016 at Yallops, in Norwich. His most recent ventures have been in travel photography.

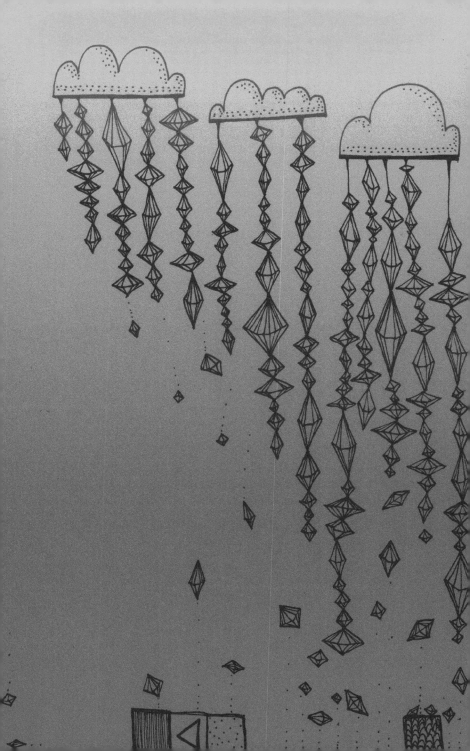